Letter To My Children

Letter To My Children

A MEMOIR

LAWRENCE M. TOMBE

Troubador Publishing Ltd
Unit E2 Airfield Business Park
Harrison Road, Market Harborough
Leicestershire LE16 7UL
Tel: 0116 279 2299
Email: books@troubador.co.uk
Web: www.troubador.co.uk

ISBN 978 1 80514 476 2

British Library Cataloguing in Publication Data.
A catalogue record for this book is available from the British Library.

Printed and bound in Great Britain by 4edge Limited
Typeset in 11pt Minion Pro by Troubador Publishing Ltd, Leicester, UK

To my children, grandchildren, the younger generation in South Sudan, and to all our departed loved ones.

Contents Table

Special Thanks

Letter To My Children is an account for conveyance of messages of love and encouragement of our children to strive for the best in life and flags out the enduring struggles of the younger generations in South Sudan in pursuance of their development goals and search of peace, despite the hardships they face.

Ideas and thoughts in putting the letter together are drawn from various sources, on the top of which were the inspirational letters my father wrote to me while he was imprisoned in the 1950s, motivated by pledges my colleagues and I made while we were in exile many decades ago that we would stay connected to our offsprings through the written word, no matter how far apart we are, and promises to myself that I would write letters to my children all along as they blossomed to adulthood.

To that end, the highest tribute in writing this letter goes to my father, who saw the value of parenting in good and trying times, and the need to enhance love within the family. My heartfelt gratitude goes to my childhood friends, companions, and cousins for the dreams we shared on how to stay closely connected to our children by all means, particularly through the spread of love and knowledge.

To my education mentors, I am deeply indebted to them for the moral norms they imparted to us for our proper growth and upbringing of our children. I profoundly thank

Professor Alfred Sebit Lokuji for inspiring me to write accounts of my life for the benefit of our children, future generations, and posterity.

I am hugely grateful to my wife, Martha Tamara Modi, for her encouragement in writing and editing the manuscript.

Our children's support in writing the letter is immensely appreciated, including the financial support they accorded in publication of the book.

Introductory Message

My Dear Children,

I intended to write handwritten letters to each one of you in the old-fashioned way all along: at your infancy, during your childhood and adult years. I failed to deliver on that promise. No excuses at all for those lapses.

This letter is put together to convey to you my love, thoughts, and captivating messages on some of the lessons drawn from my lifelong journey. Beyond that, the letter probes into societal challenges faced in troubled South Sudan – all that aimed at preparing you to live meaningfully with a purpose. By the same token, the letter conveys to you our affirmation of your amazing accomplishments earned in uncertain times.

Throughout my life, I met wonderful people who supported me in good and hard times, many of whom I associated with for the most part of my life. In certain instances, I was rescued out of life-threating situations by exceptional individuals. Over the years, I also came across people who didn't mean well to me and my family.

Although part of my lifetime journey was hard, at times brutal, I lived my life to the fullest. I refrained from dwelling on my losses, and never made a big deal on how many times I fell, as attested by the few testimonies outlined for you in this letter.

My children, you may come across similar encounters

and many more challenges that you will definitely experience. There are extraordinary people out there whom you will interact with and relate to, relationships that will stand you in good stead.

Go out there, develop yourselves, explore the universe, and live your life in accordance with your dreams and hopes. Humanity in the world thrives despite the calamities faced.

This letter encourages you to accomplish much more in life because of the greatness you are. All you need to do is to remain focused in whatever you do. Given your intellectual prowess, I am sure you are capable of adjusting to an ever-changing world, and able to separate 'vultures from kites' as you navigate yourselves in this harsh world.

The messages here are intended to inspire you to reach the summit of your dreams and hopes. And if you temporarily cannot reach mountaintops, don't give up. Pick yourselves up and move on as doors will open for you.

You are alerted here to the ongoing upheavals consuming our motherland, South Sudan. There is dire need for you, our grandchildren, and the youths in our war-torn country to stay on course in whatever you and the rest do in these trying times. Beyond war, chaos, and conflict, peace is the outcome.

You and our grandchildren, including the oppressed youths in the homeland, must seek grounds for hope in life while pursuing your education and personal development goals, even in the most difficult times. Turn inward in desperate times to revive yourselves and rely on your inner fortitude to overcome challenges confronting you.

Cultivation of your children's sense of belonging and purpose are crucial steps for advancement of their education – a development path that will help them grow up as better citizens. The letter attempts to awaken you to that inspirational and directional approach.

In recounting part of my life's journey in this letter, I am endeavouring to express to you that any turnaround of fortunes in war-torn South Sudan is possible only after the ongoing armed conflict is halted. However, the onus of that search for lasting peace in the land is passed on to you, the younger generation, since the older generation have already squandered the opportunity of accomplishing that goal.

The story here implores you to stand up for your rights and good causes. Take whatever you desire from the messages in the letter passed on to you. Use the knowledge you imbibe for the forward march. You and your generation are capable of righting the wrongs that brought you all unimaginable pains and hurt.

Above all, this letter is written for conveyance of our love to you all, our children.

1

You're Loved to Eternity

My Beloved Children,

At your birth, each one of you arrived in our midst without commands and edicts. Your infant gazes and glares radiated powerful and unbreakable bonds that brought us joy, which inspired me, in particular, to build the family I desperately longed for, which you are.

All along my life journey, I stumbled and made many mistakes; and will make many more blunders. I accept the responsibility of all past and present wrongdoings. For those imperfections, and inaccuracies, I am profoundly sorry for any hurt and pain that I might have inflicted upon you. Those blunders were made in my attempt to have you acquire the needed living tools – the moral and societal values that made you what you are today.

I am far from being the perfect father you wanted me to be – but one thing is for sure, I did the best I could to help you grow up meaningfully with a purpose in life.

The mistakes I made came from lack of understanding, but not from absence of love, because from the moment you arrived in our midst, I loved you and still love you wholeheartedly with all my might to the end.

My children, I love you more than you will ever know, now and for all eternity.

2

Unfulfilled Pledges

My Dear Children,

I thank our awesome Lord for blessing my household with you, my lovely children that I longed for. You are birth miracles that I always look back to with marvel.

Way before you arrived in our midst, I pledged – decades ago during my struggles in exile – never to expose my offspring to the horrors of war and refugee life. That covenant was taken against the backdrop of the lifetime horrors, which my generation so brutally experienced in exile.

Sadly, that promise to keep you out of harm's way was broken when we moved you into the uncertainties of war and conflict away from the homeland during your tender ages. All that I planned in my youthful years to raise my children in a stable and peaceful environment was dashed. Regrettably, we dragged you through chaos and political upheavals during those childhood years.

Moving you to the harshness of life in refuge was a gut-wrenching decision that had to be taken. Considering the worsening insecurity and intensification of the north-south armed conflict that plagued the country between 1983 and 2004, that difficult decision to take you away from the motherland to challenging living in far lands had to be taken.

In the confusions of war and the resulting human dispersal, and in the midst of the volatile politics back then, we moved you to various locations and cities within the Sudan and to faraway lands – flights from the homeland that affected stability of your young lives and smooth progress of your education. Unlike us, your parents, who returned from exile to the homeland after attainment of peace in 1972, most of you are unfortunately stuck in exile to this day.

We unintentionally exiled you in foreign countries due to the past and ongoing wars raging in South Sudan to the present day. With all the ups and downs that you faced, you nevertheless have kept to the mark in your learning endeavours wherever we settled you.

With peace prospects looking farfetched back home due to the devastating internal strife, chances of you and your children returning to the motherland soon are diminished. However, that candle of hope for your return to Africa is still burning. I am looking forward for that home return one day, in the near or distant future. In the meanwhile, we wish you well wherever you are – praying and hoping that you make the best out of your education, development, and career journeys.

For those of you internally displaced back home in Africa, I am in prayers every single day for you to overcome any untenable situations and human dispersal challenges confronting you. In any development endeavours that may confront you, try hard not to give up, as there is always a silver lining in the dark cloud.

Dear Children,

I recognise the difficult education journey that you undertook against the backdrop of your burdened past. Against those odds, you were resilient, proved your worth, and used your drive for excellence in whatever you did. That single-mindedness to reach the skies landed you to where you are today, adeptness that will propel you to gain more accolades.

Overall, you have overridden the education storms and are now managing your lives to the best of your abilities. You have shown all along in your education and career journeys that if one cannot climb a mountain, taking a longer route around it is key to success – a mantra that you all followed in overcoming your life's hurdles to the present day.

Everything that happens to you in your life, including your past ups and downs, produced you. You have drawn from the many lessons and life experiences that shaped you to the person you are today.

Continue to benefit from the lessons you learned in life for nurturing your loved ones, our grandchildren, and use the knowledge you attained in the past and acquired all along for improvement of yourselves, your offspring, and betterment of society at large.

Messages to Each One of You, My Children

My Beloved Daughter, Lurit,

In your infant years as I carried and sat you on my lap, I saw a lovely daughter in the image of my mother, your grandmother, Mama Lucia Lurit Tumöŋ Na'Musö. You are immensely loved, a daughter raised well with love.

Your pre-school years were a great joy to follow. Years of separation from this household did not obstruct your determination to stay connected to the family, nor did it prevent you from pursuing your educational goals despite the hard learning journey you undertook. Despite those challenges, you focused on your learning and personal development with utmost determination and carried on with your education to the finish. You made us proud of you.

You settled down to family life well and are doing exceedingly well in raising your lovely children to their full potential in accordance with our family values and norms.

With the amazing writing skills you possess, the family has a writer and an author in the making. I look forward to seeing you translate those lofty language abilities to written works. Use your script talents to tell your own stories, which will greatly contribute to knocking off the single narratives told about you and the rest of the family by outsiders.

"There is no greater agony than bearing an untold story

inside you." I didn't say that. Maya Angelou – the American memoirist and poet – did. Tell your story for the benefit of yourself, the family, and the community at large.

Lurit, you and Lucia are gift daughters from above, representing the mother I only had glimpses of when I was an infant – a birth mother incarnated in the likeliness of both of you.

Your love, kindness, and understanding that overflows is the quintessence of that motherly love I so badly missed. I am proud of you both in providing the leadership this family is yearning for.

"Thank you, Mama Lucia Lurit, wholeheartedly, for blessing your granddaughters and all my offspring."

My Dear Lucia Wasuk,

I watched you sail off fast at the slightest learning breeze that blew in your direction during your early schooling at the Juba Model School. And when you progressed in your education, you excelled all through. You recall, Lucia, the private Arabic tuition you had that brought you up to the needed linguistic levels – a mandatory requirement at the time for taking the Sudan secondary school leaving exams. Overcoming those language barriers, you positioned yourself within the top pack at the Khartoum Sisters' School back in the 1980s.

Solidly grounded in your early schooling, your well-nurtured capabilities readied you for advance learning in the later years. You deserve the scholastic achievements that came your way. With all the accolades you gathered over the years – and still garnering more in your lofty professional career – you have made us proud of you for all those accomplishments.

Dear Emmanuel, Tombe, Henry, George, Rhoda, Edward,

We took delight in every learning pathway all of you went through in those pre-school and primary learning years. That solid education foundation prepared all of you well for advancement of your education down the years. Thereon, you all were not daunted by the schooling hurdles you laboured through – from the English system of education to the Arabic pedagogy you transitioned into when we moved you away from Juba to Khartoum in the mid-1980s.

Even the afternoon classes that you attended in the scorching North Sudan heat didn't destroy your learning yearnings. You adapted so well to the Arabic pattern of learning that left doubters dumbfounded. With every learning step that you took, you said, 'I can do it', and you did it.

For every unsettling move taken to get you away from harm, all of you endured those difficult education journeys. You turned those learning uncertainties into rainbow clouds. Down the years, all of you reached your educational goals, and positioned yourselves on the mountain summit like mahogany trees perched on a mountaintop.

You are an embodiment of education excellence obtained under harsh and unpredictable conditions. You have shown that nothing under the sun can impede you from attaining your education and career goals.

Through your steadfastness and determination to climb the scholastic and career ladders, thus far, you have proved that you can do hard things to reach and stay at the top. Well done for your achievements, for being you, and for making us prouder of you all.

My Dear Emmanuel, Henry, Rhoda,

All of you, along with Lucia, are pacemakers that set the professional and career high bars this family is so proud of. Thank you all for pursuing your dreams and for reaching the top. Continue to add on to the accolades you already earned and are still navigating to more desired goals.

Leading from the front that way, I am proud of every one of you for not fearing the unknown in trying to reach the skies – heights that will lead you to gaining many more honours that will be added to your outstanding accomplishments.

My Dear Tombe,

This is to let you know that we love you immensely – love that grows by the day. Tombe, son, you are an essential and integral part of this family that everyone in this household adores. Stay connected to the family because everyone needs you, to draw from your amazing love and charisma, which is missed so much by us all.

You're part of that very minute percentage of the human race striving to rid our planet of sin, wars, and strife – essential endeavours that are part of the long Christian journey to sustainable following of God's ways, which the human race is longing for.

I am proud of your devotion to the Christian faith. This family is blessed to have you, one of us, who ploughs his capabilities towards betterment of humanity. Thank you, Tombe, for being part of the Christian battle for making our world a better place to live in.

Remember, Tombe, you are loved immensely and unconditionally by us all in the family; we are looking forward to welcoming you home anytime, all the time. As an integral part of this family, I believe you cannot stay away from home forever without connecting with us.

You're part of this family's dreams and hopes that you carry under your skin and lodged at the extreme corner of your eyes, and which is permanently edged in your being.

Stay connected to the family, Tombe, and come home whenever you can under no pressure! We love you to eternity.

My Dear George,

You have gone through a lot in your young life, and all along you bounced back from your life's trials to resounding successes. Your resilience, fortitude, and determination to reach your set education and development goals are sole drivers that all the time propel you to the top. Thanks to your unyielding resolve to move on in hard and good times.

Congratulations, George, for attaining your postgraduate degree with flying colours. The entire family applaud your outstanding success that proves your academic competence.

Well done for adding more to your professional achievements. Keep raising the scholastic bar on yourself. The skies are the limit of that educational and professional journey.

Edward, my son,

I recall your school and university years in which your learning talents were discovered, and the opportunities opened for your scholastic advancement. Remember, Edward: I used to drive you to the university at the beginning of each semester. During those return-to-campus trips, we shared a lot of ideas about your education dreams and career plans. Your future was so promising, still is up to now.

Remember the little but important things that you and I shared: shopping for your food items; orderly arrangement of those ration packages in your kitchen shelves in your apartment; and our discussions on preparations of your meals. Given your amazing personality, both of us joked and laughed on sharing many interesting thoughts. Those conversations showed your intellectual prowess on many knowledge fronts.

Edward, son – you are one of our gifted children with a very high IQ, one that was measured in the past on one of the professional scales. Even in the most trying times of your illnesses and during your bedridden struggles, you continued to display excellence in positive thinking. While bedridden, you oftentimes delved into reading books written by great minds: the likes of Emmanuel Kant; Barton Russell; Roger Scruton; and many more titles.

Flashing back on the book purchases I conducted at your request, I delivered those titles to you while you were very ill at Royal Free Hospital. Fascinated by Roger Scruton's works that you introduced to me, I acquired one title for myself.

You have an outstanding mind, Edward. I am proud of the genius in you waiting to be exploited. Given your determination to live, I am sure you will achieve many well-being and intellectual goals.

Right from start of your serious ailments in 2006, you

fought the health menaces with amazing courage. Although you didn't come to terms with your health conditions initially, you adjusted to normal life like others not daunted by similar health issues.

Your amazing resilience, courage, and determination to live on, are character traits that greatly helped you to overcome your healing hurdles to the present day. All along, we, your parents, are standing by your side every step of the way, Edward – on good days and bad days.

We implore you to remain focused. Although you are trying your level best in managing your treatment and medication, you need to do more in this direction. Do not give up trying to live a normal life. Follow your medication intake as required; and follow the doctors' instructions for enhancement of your health and wellness.

Edward, know that all you need to better your life is in you. Use your outstanding capabilities to turn your surmountable health misfortunes to accomplishment of your desired goals. We in the family know that you are conversant about the road to your full recovery; and are equally aware that you are cognisant of the abundant opportunities out there awaiting for your taking.

All of us in the family are standing by your side in your struggles with your illnesses. You are always in our hearts and we are behind you 100%. You can get through this, Edward. We are right here for you.

We are so lucky to have you in our lives. Above all, know that you are immensely loved by us all in the family.

4

My Infancy Begins

I was born in Juba Hospital in February 1948. After three months, or there about, Mama Lucia Lurit Tumöŋ Musö (my birthmother) took me to Lotiama sub-village – my maternal ancestral home in Gondokoro Village.

That visit to my maternal roots turned out to be Mama Lucia's last before she took her last breath – a devasting passing on of my mother that marked the beginning of my hard journey in life. That was the cruellest misfortune faced by a three-month infant tossed into an uncertain world caused by mother's death. I was too little to grasp the serious implications of that tragic passing on of Mama Lurit.

My mother breastfed me in her last moments before she died. In death, Mom held me tightly until I was removed from her earthly remains, I was told. No one knew for how long I clung to Mama Lucia, breastfeeding me undisturbed after she was long gone to the afterlife.

No one around knew how and when my mother died. It was only the Almighty God above that marked my mother's last moments before her death. I learned from my maternal uncles much later that my mother passed on peacefully in the quietness of the night.

Mama Lurit's silent bye-bye to me was stamped by that bodily contact before I was removed. The mother-to-infant ultimate love was already bonded at those tragic moments – transcended to levels beyond me.

A few days after my mother's death, I was handed over to my stepmother, Mama Anyeze Kiteŋ, who miraculously lactated while ingeniously trying to breastfeed me. Mama Kiteŋ raised me well – an adopted stepson – before she gave birth to her elder son, my brother, Peter Toŋun Tombe.

I was nourished by that stepmother's milk until I blossomed into a healthy and strong infant. No one understood that smooth breastfeeding and motherly transition, except the powers above. I strongly believe Mama Lucia, my birth mother – through direction of our awesome God – guided me into the motherly hands of Mama Anyeze Kiteŋ.

I am sure Mama Lucia watched over me from those infant beginnings onward and throughout the challenging years and stayed by my side to the present day.

Sixty years ago in 1963, I was miraculously saved from death by an unknown person that I later thought was guided by the Heavens above through my 'guardian angel'. That miracle started with a car park attendant pulling me out from a taxi – first car in the queue, waiting to travel towards my school situated along the Kampala-Entebbe Road, approximately twenty-four kilometres away from Kampala City.

My seat in the cab was given to a favoured passenger – an extremely brusque removal from the cab that made me furious. I protested against that outrageous ejection from the taxi, but in vain. I didn't know why I was singled out not to travel in that manner.

After a while, I was offered a seat in the next taxi about to drive off. Our car immediately followed that taxi I was extracted from, which overturned under our watch, a short distance away from the car park, on the Kampala-Entebbe motorway – a tragic accident that killed all the passengers on board.

Instinctively, I considered my removal from the overturned taxi a miracle, and a divine intervention. I strongly felt my late mother had a hand in sending the car park attendant – the magnanimous angel – that saved my life by pulling me out of that taxi before it drove off to its fatal end. It was definitely a miracle that I attributed to the powers above and Mama Lucia.

Mesmerised by that life-saving incident, I could not pull myself together to absorb what happened that day. Arriving safely at my school that afternoon, it took me a long time to settle down to classes. I continued my schooling at St Mary's till I joined Makerere University. From then on, I knew Mama Lucia Lurit provided the pillar that I leaned on over the years. I strongly feel my mother stands by my side in my hours of need to this day.

Throughout my early childhood, I had always wished for the resurrection of my mom – birth mother longings that linger on to the present times. It is that invincible motherly love and support that inspired me to complete my education, which enabled me thereon to raise my lovely children.

I know the Almighty God has rested Mama Lucia's soul in eternal peace and in the choicest place in Heaven.

5

The Mango Paradise

After completing his education in Okaru Intermediate School in 1934, my father started his civil service employment in Juba Town; afterwards transferred to Yei Municipality as head staff clerk. Afterwards, he served in Nagichot, a sub-district in Kapoeta District, Eastern Equatoria, and afterwards returned to Juba where he ended his long government service in 1953 that spanned eighteen years.

Back in those days, any government employee serving at the administrative level was compelled by the colonial government to work in any part of the Sudan, and required to take up new assignments at short notice. My father conformed to those reallocation arrangements – the reason why he was transferred to several administrative locations over his public service career in Equatoria Province.

On his transfer to start his new assignment in Yei Municipality – one hundred miles away from Juba Town – my father obliged and left for Yei River District with his family in fulfilment of that government order. At that early stage of my infancy, I was not aware about that family move out of Juba to Yei. I did not remember much in those tender years about the actual road trip to Yei Town – except for the bumpy road that rocked me to sleep for most of the truck journey.

On arrival at the outskirts of the municipality, I vividly recall the Yei River's dazzling bridge that we crossed. The fruit-laden mango trees that lined both sides of the road seemed an organised spectacle to welcome us to the town centre. I watched the outline of the mango trees with wonder. Most of the mango trees along the road had ripe fruit drooping down, as if calling to be collected.

The truck finally came to a halt in front of a brick house with grass-thatched roof, a government residence that looked enormous to my child's eyes. That house became our home over our stay in Yei. The lushness of the fruit trees: mangoes, oranges, lemons, and papayas surrounding our new home was, to me, a scene out of this planet.

The entire municipality was garlanded by mango trees, street by street, and within residential compounds. The small urban sprawl and its surroundings was full of mango trees. To my young eyes, I concluded that the abundance of the mango trees in the district was a 'Mango Paradise'.

Mango trees are domestic trees grown all over Yei River District, and across other agricultural heartlands in South Sudan, nurtured, well-tended, and owned by the citizens in those territories. In the Yei motherland, the 'Mango Paradise' is a territory of hard-working and productive farmers, and law-abiding citizens. This fruit tree adorns homesteads and the surrounding countryside.

Its mystical value galvanises the oneness and unity of the populations growing the tree across South Sudan. The mango tree denotes rural tranquillity and prosperity generated by the farmers who plant and continue to spread it. Under its cool shade, stability amongst the peace-loving populations in Yei River District is reinforced. To date, many people from near and faraway lands are attracted to this phenomenal mango heaven in Yei River District.

Mango trees are not grown in the wilderness on their own, as claimed by the land grabbers and territorial invaders. Everyone, including the current prophets of doom and enablers of evil, should remember that the pure calmness and magical powers of the mango tree are conclaves under which differences and disputes are settled, and sustainable peace is attained in hard times.

The magnetic attraction of the mango tree draws youngsters and urban dwellers alike back to their ancestral roots over vacations and during festive visits. Mango trees are fondly revered by children in Equatoria for their fruits, and for their power to bring back happy moments and memories. It is that mango mystic that evokes my unforgettable memories about Yei, wedged in my mind forever.

'Mango Paradise' – "I implore you to assist the people in this our motherland to do what's right – right that they must do for the sake of peace. Your mystical powers are forever."

Another feature of Yei Town that stuck in my mind to this day, was the presence of tamed elephants brought to the municipality from the Belgian Congo at the end of every year for entertainment purposes during the Christmas festive seasons.

The mere size of the mighty elephants was an overwhelming spectacle to a young kid of my age. During those Christmas festivities, game warders rode on the backs of the gentle beasts during circus shows organised in the municipality public square.

The gigantic animals were ordered around by way of verbal directions and through use of batons to perform well-choreographed feats. The kings of the forest responded by doing acrobatic manoeuvres, flapping their enormous ears while moving their heavy tusks from side to side with ease – scenes that tremendously fascinated me and the other children.

Reflecting on those Christmas extravaganzas, I am always reminded of the lovely times of my early childhood in Yei – unforgettable occasions etched in my mind forever.

Although we only resided in Yei Town for two years, that short stay was memorable. The spectacular beauty of Yei Town, including its surrounding counties and the beautiful landscape, are huge tourist attractions, and potential awaiting utilisation. The 'Mango Paradise' shall remain forever.

6

Nagichot

On leaving Yei on my father's transfer to Nagichot sub-district (the present Budi County in Eastern Equatoria) in Kapoeta District, we stopped over in Juba briefly for my father to plan for the eastbound journey that materialised a week after.

As our truck sped away towards the Juba Pontoon Ferry at the start of our long journey to Nagichot, I saw our family dog, Kulu ko Ngun, chasing the lorry to catch up with us. 'They are with God' was an English version of our dog's name. I cried out, calling, "Kulu ko Ngun, Kulu ko Ngun," when I saw our beautiful dog desperately racing after us! Our truck sped away, as if trying to outrun Kulu ko Ngun. I was totally floored by the abandonment of our dog that I was so fond of.

No one in the lorry seemed bothered about my yelling for rescue of the family dog. Although emotionally attached to Kulu ko Ngun, I was helpless in getting him join the travelling party. After a while, our little dog was outraced and was, sadly, out of sight. Tears swelled in my eyes. I sobbed quietly not to draw the attention of my parents, and more for fear of being noticed crying.

Any child's cry for such juvenile demands – considered unnecessary by the adults in the family – was met with the rod. Just imagine the approach to child discipline back then!

Those were the old ways that children back then had to put up with. To stay clear of corporal discipline, children in our family made sure they stayed away from trouble. That's exactly what I avoided over my cry for Kulu ko Ngun. I didn't want to annoy my parents on that long eastbound journey.

Despite the strict discipline and the structured life curbed for us by our parents, children in our family came to terms with that way of life. The rod discipline aside, we knew our parents loved us – contrary to today's world where such approaches in child-rearing are narrowed down to child abuse.

Those parental ways of child upbringing were done for inculcation of the African ways and moral values. The 1940s and 1950s generation of youngsters in our part of the world, that I was part of, were mentored under that stern social order. In a sense, we were forged out of strict disciplines – African norms that shaped me to the adult I am today.

Back to the Kulu ko Ngun saga, I couldn't get my head around why our family dog was not with us on our journey to Nagichot. Was he deliberately left behind? Or was he away from home at the time of our departure? So many unanswered questions ran through my mind. As children's whining about their problems – oftentimes regarded petty – was not allowed in our family, I retreated and kept quiet till the pontoon boat ferried us to the other side of River Nile.

On boarding the truck at the start of our eastbound journey, the agonising thoughts of Kulu ko Ngun had already faded away from my mind. My attention from then onward was diverted to the happenings at the bank of the river and the journey ahead of us.

We arrived Nagichot as scheduled. Much cooler than Yei, Nagichot is scenic with a staggering mountainous environment – the 'Didinga' mountain range. With its cool and rainy weather, Nagichot sub-district is an agricultural territory endowed with a variety of agricultural products, including crops and fruits brought from the western world that grew very well there.

Many years later, after my return home from exile, I had an urge of asking my father why Kulu ko Ngun, the family dog, didn't travel with us to Nagichot then. I refrained from pursuing the issue, as my father was too sick and fragile to be engaged on such childhood matters long gone.

However, those juvenile thoughts about desertion of our lovely dog lingered on in my mind to this day. A sense of guilt about that neglect haunts me to this very day. As emotionally attached to Kulu ko Ngun as I was, I am still saddened for turning our backs to our lovely dog when we moved to Nagichot without him.

Surrounded by the Didinga mountain range, Nagichot Town was beautiful and blessed with evergreen vegetation and mountainous foliage. I ate my first strawberries in Nagichot, temperate climate fruits that grew around our residential block and in parts of the small town.

Once more, I came across another fruit heaven similar to Yei Town's mango tree abundance. My childhood fascination with Nagichot's greenery made me describe the sub-district as another fruit heaven. The British administrators in charge of the sub-district back then must have taken strawberry seeds/seedlings to the municipality, probably at the beginning of the colonial adventures in that part of Eastern Equatoria.

The Assistant District Commissioner (ADC) residence, perched on a hilltop, was a towering mansion that overlooked the small urban centre downhill. We, children, imagined the ADC residence as a place that would have swallowed us children, if we got close to it.

That childish fear about the mansion was reinforced by our parents who told us that bad people living in the building would have snatched and taken us away to far lands for good, if we strayed to the building.

Did our parents warn us to stay away from that imposing house bearing in mind the slave extractions that happened on the Africa continent centuries ago? Or was it simply a parents' scare to keep us away from the ADC mansion? I didn't know.

The answers to these questions are ingrained in the past horrors about the brutal plunders of the land by the foreign slavers and invaders. Our fears regarding the ADC mansion were drawn from the stories we heard in Yei about the kulia batu – the purportedly man-eating white people of the Belgian Congo that kidnapped people in town on every festive occasion.

According to those tales pedalled in Yei in the colonial past, the so-called 'man eaters' of the Belgian Congo used powerful torches that duped and lured their victims to capture traps. Those scary thoughts groping in our young minds were the reason why we kept away from the ADC's imposing building. No children ever ventured towards that menacing-looking building beyond the confines of our housing estate. I left Nagichot without getting closer to that official residence.

I returned to Nagichot decades after for short visits. To my disappointment, the ADC's mansion was no more on that hilltop, a reminder of the colonial past that should have been preserved for historical reasons. Although much of the colonial landmarks in Nagichot Town – including the ADC mansion – were all gone, my memories about the town are stuck in that 1950s past.

7

School Vacations at Our Ancestral Homes

I was availed abundant opportunities – in the course of my early childhood – to make visits to my uncles in Gondokoro and Bilinyang villages over our school breaks. I was equally given the chance to spend part of the school vacations at my stepmother's home in Kit Village, Nyarbanga County, and in Sindiru Village – my father's ancestral home. Over the long holidays, I stayed at 'Pager' Village – our rural home in Lo'bonok County, Southern Bari.

I frequently spent the mid-term school breaks with paternal uncles at Burödu Village, part of the present Bilinyang County. Situated along 'Wangar' River – fifteen miles away from Juba Town – Burödu had an ideal play environment for children back in the 1950s. Wangar River had beautiful sand beds that children played on and exercised their wrestling skills during the dry-season months. The surrounding riverbanks and countryside were teeming with orchards of extensive mango, guava, lemon, and papaya trees, including sweet potato, cassava, and vegetable gardens.

Besides the exquisite playgrounds that kept me busy with the rest of my village cousins, it was a joy staying in Burödu Village with my paternal Uncle Tombe Ködöŋ, Auntie Parasede Ködöŋ, and the rest of the relatives who accorded me all their love over those short school holidays.

Visiting my maternal uncles at Gondokoro Village during those learning breaks were occasions full of memorable treats. Unlike Burödu, Gondokoro Village is an extensive territory made up of many sub-villages along the river Nile, including Lotiama sub-village, my birth mother's home and final resting place.

Over my stays at Gondokoro, I occasionally paid visits to Lue, an island sub-village, part of which belonged to my maternal uncles. Lue Island is the main market gardening source for my uncles, producing cash crops sold in the Juba grocery markets. Up to the present time, farm gardening and fishing are the main agricultural activities carried out in the island.

In the past, Lue provided greener pastures to the local livestock brought to the island during the dry season months. Those seasonal cattle raring activities are long gone due to perennial theft of livestock by pastoralists hailing from Bor, Jonglei Region in Upper Nile State – pillage that led to eradication of the local stocks.

Livestock rearing – which at the time was part of my uncles' source of livelihood – is no more due to that systemic looting of the local cattle. The indigenous livestock were wiped out, aggravated by the use of arms gotten through connivance of those in power; heinous crimes committed with impunity that led to impoverishment of farmers in Bari land.

In recent years after South Sudan attained its sovereignty, unlawful occupation of indigenous territories in the Equatoria heartlands was stepped up as a result of weaponisation of the pastoralists. Those territorial invasions were enforced as a matter of policy by those in power for purposes of expansionist drives.

Over my short stays at Lue Island during the school breaks, I was fascinated with the hook-and-net methods of fishing undertaken on traditional canoes. Oftentimes challenged by my village cousins, I bravely attempted fishing on the home boats. To do that, one had to paddle a canoe as a first step in boat fishing, waterways skills that I failed miserably to acquire. In those fishing expeditions, I painfully watched my cousins carry out fishing activities without my participation. Not keeping up with the boat-fishing challenge, I was utterly disappointed by that failure.

On other occasions, I took chances with line fishing on the banks of the Nile that oftentimes ended in no takeaways. Returning home without catches while my village cousins carried away plenty of fish was the most disappointing experience I had.

Uncle Tombe Musö came to my rescue by comforting me after those unsuccessful fishing trials and saying that I was a big fisherman in the making, and added that all my cousins were worse off than me when they started the fish harvesting trade. That consolation was comforting. I loved Uncle Tombe for his understanding and kindness. He was a huge motivator.

Overall, my maternal uncles: Chief Legge Tombe, the paramount chief of Gondokoro Village; Uncle Tombe Musö; Uncle Enyaso Ngwanki Lo'Sugga; and many other younger uncles all accorded me unparalleled love over those holiday visits to Gondokoro. On returning to town for resumption of classes, I always looked forward for the next vacations in the countryside.

Many of my lovely uncles passed on over the years. Let the Almighty God rest their souls in eternal peace. Uncle Bureng

Musö, my mother's elder brother; Uncle Legge Tombe; Uncle Enyaso Ngwanki Lo'Sugga, who passed away in the recent past; and many other late uncles are greatly missed. Sadly, many of my beloved uncles passed on to afterlife in my absence. I remember them all for providing me with the pillar to lean on over my difficult childhood years.

Blessed with a large extended family, I spent part of my short and long school breaks at Kit sub-village – my stepmother's home in Karpeto, Nyarbanga County in Southern Bari. Back then, my two brothers (the late Peter Loro Tombe and the late Patrick Lodu Tombe) and I loved visiting Kit Village during our school vacations, visits undertaken in company of Mama Anyeze Kiteng, my stepmother.

Kit sub-village – located sixty kilometres away from Juba town on the Juba-Nimule highway – is part of Karpeto Village in Nyarbanga County, Southern Bari. Positioned between Kit and Nyolok rivers, Kit was my rural dream home, a lovely geographical location with excellent weather and fantastic playgrounds for children.

All that a child wanted to do outdoors was there in Kit Village. The village was endowed with amazing swimming spots on the two rivers (Kit and Nyolok). That fascinating countryside had out-of-this-world tree climbing settings for childhood adventures in the wild; extensive playing fields; bird hunting sceneries; and above all, plenty of fruit varieties to feast on.

During those stays in the village, our cousins and us, along with the other children in the village, played endlessly in the playgrounds around Kit Elementary School, and elsewhere within the village. Those scenic and amazing locations are now gone. The entire village is now illegally occupied by property looters and territorial grabbers – land looting and extortions enabled through excessive use of arms. Sadly, that level of land theft is presently worsened through connivance of those in power.

Occasionally, we spent our school breaks at Sindiru Village, our ancestral home where my father was born, but used up most of the vacation period at 'Pager' Village, our paternal home in Lo'bonok County, Southern Bari. After the Christmas celebrations in Juba, the family moved to Pager to spend the rest of the festive season there. To us children, those retreats to our rural home in Southern Bari were the best way of spending the remaining part of the school holidays.

There were lots of activities for children and grown-ups at Pager Village. Our village cousins had the habit of challenging us to a football match straight away on our arrival to the village. They wanted to test whatever new game skills we brought from town. We obliged but with very unimpressive skills.

What I loved most was our tour of the extensive cultivation fields and orchards around the homesteads teeming with mango, guava, orange, lemon, and papaya, and other indigenous fruits that we feasted on. Apart from that, we ravaged the countryside for play opportunities. We loved tree climbing, played hide-and-seek games, and learned how to fish using locally made fishing hooks and rods. We explored the surroundings endlessly, and at times went hunting for guinea fowls and rabbits.

Above all, we spent most of our time in the family farms where we were taught how to harvest groundnuts, cassava, and sweet potatoes, and shown how to roast sweet potatoes in open ovens called *matafali*, miniature kilns made of chunks of soil and burnt red-hot for the roasting. Sweet potatoes roasted in that way were amazingly tasty, much tastier roasts than the ones baked in modern ovens.

A more fascinating event was fire-making, lit out of sticks. The fire-making tools consisted of a stick cut to a dull point and a grooved piece of larger wood. We would spend hours trying to produce the hot dust and embers by pressing the twig hard and rubbing it down the wooden groove. It is that consistent downward ploughing motion that produced the glowing fire.

Creation of the fire glows was a thrill to obtain and watch. The fire-making expertise of our village cousins was admiringly employed in production of the flames – a process done through careful fanning of the embers. We, the town kids, failed to acquire those captivating fire-making skills, no matter how much and how long we tried. Nonetheless, we were always proud of being part of the fire-making team.

Those incredible sweet-potato roasting occasions and the fire-creation resourcefulness were experiences – among other fascinations in the village – that drew us back to Pager Village at the end of every year during our long school vacations. Reminiscing about that childhood past, I am overwhelmed with waves of nostalgia.

My father, a wildlife hunter, had a licensed magnum rifle and a double-barrel shotgun, both used on hunting expeditions that he organised with the local hunters in the village. While the rifle was utilised for hunting big game like elephants, buffalos, antelopes, and gazelles, the shotgun was used for shooting smaller animals like guinea fowls and bush rabbits.

In the 1950s, a game license was issued by the Department of Wildlife. A specificised number of animals were allotted to a hunter per year: three elephants, twelve buffaloes, and so on. The number of animals approved for hunting were given in proportion to existing stocks in the wild.

My father and the local hunters in the village would go hunting in the bushes, expeditions that usually lasted for days or weeks. At the end of any long hunting period, the hunting party would return to the village with a lot of bush meat. Occasionally, elephant tusks were brought in the mix, which back then signified a very successful hunting season. Each ivory was carried by two or three porters, depending on the weight of each tusk. The elephant trophies fetched a lot of money in the commercial market in those days.

I was fascinated by those hunting expeditions. As I grew older, I pleaded to my father to allow me to join the hunting parties that he organised during the 1954 to 1956 hunting seasons. Eventually, I was allowed to partake in one of those hunting excursions. Since I was still a juvenile, I was well protected in those ventures into the wild.

I was fascinated by those hunting expeditions. Those hunting adventures required hunters' alertness, bravery, and strict adherence to safety responsibilities. A renown hunter in the Bari Community is revered and placed high in the social hierarchy after rainmakers – accorded the highest social standings in the land like Pitya Lugör, the King of the Bari rainmakers.

My visits to the rural areas over the school vacations in those early years were great and enduring opportunities full of memorable experiences, which positively shaped my outlook towards life as I developed into an adult. Staying connected that way to my rural roots and traditional ways was the best thing that happened to my life.

Sharing with our loved ones in our rural homes through those memorable back-to-the-roots trips greatly widened my scope about the rich cultural and traditional ways of life that I am proudly identifying with to date as an African. I have since paid endless visits to our ancestral homes and am emotionally linked to the rural life up to now. I hope you, my children, and grandchildren, will benefit from those rich cultural opportunities in the future, once there is turnaround of fortunes in South Sudan.

This account of my early life is, to a large extent, a testimony of the beautiful life that I lived, experienced, and enjoyed during my formative years – a social order that was a source of stability and love back then, but one that is now shattered by the ongoing bitter conflict in the motherland.

In this little account of my life's story, I never thought South Sudan would one day be reduced to its present lowest point through conflict and disorder. However, I would like you – my children and grandchildren – to draw lessons from the experiences outlined here to better your lives.

Above all, know that there is a motherland for you and your children – lands of your forefathers that you should proudly identify with, which hopefully will be liberated for you to return to in the near or distant future.

8

Tribute to Our 1955 Fallen Heroes

My Dear Children,

South Sudan is currently at war with itself, reduced to ashes, caused by failure of leadership, ethnic hegemonism and state disorder to frightening levels. At these very hard times, I am reminded of our heroes and heroines who paid the ultimate price for our freedom – martyrdom that kicked off the liberation struggle in our historical past, and which the current leaders in South Sudan chose to rubbish.

As a generation heavily impacted by past wars in the old Sudan, and deeply affected by the internal strife tearing South Sudan apart presently, there is a fundamental need for you – the younger generation in the motherland – to appreciate the early stages of our liberation struggle. That knowledge will greatly help you to complete the unfinished march to the promised land, which we, the older generation, sadly failed to accomplish.

As you, our children, have come of age, it is befitting to tell you the story of the beginnings of our freedom struggle – a narrative passed on to you through the following passage dedicated to our fallen heroes of 1955. Imbibing the core values of those freedom struggles is essential for the cultivation of your sense of belonging and enhancement of your growth and participation in the promotion of good causes.

Two weeks into July 1955, classes at Kator Elementary School, where I was learning, were abruptly ended. Rumours about imminent war in Southern Sudan (as our country was known back then) was thick in the air, the beginning of our liberation struggle that was beyond my understanding at that early stage of my life.

As children are normally happy to get out of classes at the slightest pretext that comes their way, we at Kator Elementary School welcomed the learning break and happily went home, not bothered about the implications of what we heard from our teachers about the looming conflict.

War? What war? we wondered. Shrugging the war gossip off, we schoolchildren in our block settled down to what we at the time did best: play, play, and play. Contrary to that, the grownups in our family – who, of course, knew more about the looming war, insecurity, and the dangers that lay ahead of us – were ruminating over the best exit routes in case war broke out, which occurred a few weeks after.

The war between the Southern and Northern forces broke out in Torit, Eastern Equatoria, on 18 August 1955. Northern Sudanese soldiers who escaped the fighting reached Juba a few hours later. Their arrival in town triggered the heavy shooting in the government garrisons that continued for hours on end. An eerie silence followed when the sound of heavy guns stopped.

All market centres and shops in town were instantaneously closed and deserted at the outbreak of the fighting. Ordered to stay indoors by our parents, we children stayed in the limits of our homes expecting the worst to happen. Over that home confinement, I overheard my parents' discussions on how the family should leave Juba Town for the village. That difficult decision to run away to the countryside was taken in the absence of my father, who was in Khartoum at the time undertaking his parliamentary duties.

Following the heightened insecurity in Juba, the town dwellers streamed out of town to their respective villages for refuge. A few days later, the city was virtually emptied of its inhabitants. Our family joined the fleeing populations by escaping for safety to Gondokoro Village, my maternal uncles' homeland.

We stayed away in the village at the height of the military revolt, and only returned to Juba in October 1955. I hardly got a full grasp of the armed conflict, which subsequently spread to all parts of Southern Sudan – a bitter strife that down the years lasted for seventeen years, from 1955 to 1972.

Our return to Juba in November 1955 was followed by the birth of my brother, the late Wani Tombe. Although brother Wani's arrival in our midst was a welcomed and an exciting event, the family had hardly settled down to normal life due to the worsening insecurity, and on account of the stepped-up repression of citizens in Southern Sudan following the military uprising. However, semblance of normalcy returned to Juba City in the first quarter of 1956.

A worrying and heartrending situation occurred one morning when the citizens in Juba town started to witness convoys of military trucks arriving town carrying ex-soldiers that were involved in the Torit Army Uprising, brought in captivity for military trials. The transportation of the captured fighters, driven from Torit to Juba, was a daily occurrence that lasted up to the second quarter of 1956.

The arrival of our imprisoned heroes drew large crowds to the Juba Ferry-Malakia Road to witness for themselves the heartbreaking spectacle. Little as I was, I was part of that crowd that witnessed those sorrowful scenes of our liberation fighters brought to town in caged military lorries – painful experiences that remained in my mind to date.

Gripped by childlike curiosity, I occasionally joined the large crowds that assembled outside the high-walled Juba Prison to witness for myself the marching away of the jailed ex-soldiers to the military courts and taken back to custody after the summary trials. Our liberation heroes were marched, platoon by platoon, to the military court set up in the Juba District Town Hall for the botched-up trials.

After those kangaroo courtmartials, three hundred of our freedom fighters were sentenced to death, with the rest condemned to long prison sentences. One cannot forget those depressing and painful developments. The ex-combatants condemned to death were summarily executed by firing squad at the foot of Körök Mountain (dubbed *Jebel Kujur* in colloquial Arabic) on the Juba-Yei motorway.

With those heart-aching killings, the citizens in the city agonisingly heard loud gun shots that echoed in the wake of those executions, as our national heroes fell. They paid the ultimate price for the freedom of South Sudan. Many citizens in Juba Town wept openly over those sad endings of our liberation heroes. In those my tender years, I found myself wrapped up in the tempo and pains of the liberation struggle that my generation brutally endured over the first war years (1955–1972).

Of the 1,770-strong No. 2 Battalion soldiers jailed, the majority of them were imprisoned. Many of the ex-fighters died in captivity due to brutal treatment, harshness of prison life and the extreme weather conditions in Northern Sudan.

Sir Alexander Knox Helm, the last British colonial Governor General in Sudan (1954–1955), exploited the blind trust 'Southerners' had in the colonial establishment by convincing our freedom fighters to end the 1955 revolt by laying down their arms. Sir Knox Helm's connivance with the Northern Sudanese rulers led to surrender of Commander Rinaldo Loyelo, leader of the army uprising.

The British colonial governor of Sudan earned that capitulation of a dedicated freedom fighter, Commander Rinaldo Loyelo, by telling him that Prime Minister Ismail Al-Azhari had promised to accord him and his soldiers a full and fair investigation leading to their pardon if they surrendered unconditionally. Sir Knox gave his assurances to that false Azhari's testimony, which he intentionally did not honour.

Not bothered about the serious implications of the Governor General's collusion with Prime Minister Azhari against the South, Rinaldo handed himself to the enemy troops and signed the surrender terms on 28 August 1955. He, along with the other liberation soldiers, was sent to the death row on Sir Knox Helm's empty promises. That betrayal of trust caused the mass surrender of our freedom fighters, followed by the devastating halt of the liberation uprising in Southern Sudan back then.

At that early stage of my life, I wondered why our freedom fighters capitulated so easily to the enemy, only to end up in the death gallows in the way they did. Back then, I understood nothing of the complexities that surrounded that total surrender of our freedom fighters to the Northern Sudanese soldiers.

Equally disillusioned about the total submission of the

Southern army to the Northern troops, the people of South Sudan back then wondered why their freedom heroes so easily laid down their arms in that manner without putting up a fight against the Northern Sudanese army.

Many factors contributed to those fatal hesitations. Answers to those blunders are lodged in the total trust the people of South Sudan had in the British colonial masters. Back then, 'Southerners' entertained the idea that Britain, a Christian nation, was in support of the Christian cause in Southern Sudan. That naive and casual outlook in our relationship with Britain was the Achilles heel that negatively impacted our liberation struggle at the time and in the following years. That fatal misjudgement of the colonial intentions in Southern Sudan that cascaded down to us was a costly price of naivety that continues to haunt the people of South Sudan to the present day.

The outgoing colonial masters and the new rulers of Sudan worked together in laying the basis of Northern Sudanese dominance of politics and power in post-independent Sudan. The people of South Sudan paid dearly for the false hopes in our so-called external friends, who prepared the Northern Sudanese to rule the Sudan without participation of Southern Sudanese.

The unfounded trust in 'our British friends' were costly blunders that resulted in massive human loss, which set back the clock of the liberation struggle in Southern Sudan at the time. The sum total of those calculated schemes against the South was the reason why the people of South Sudan opted for the armed struggle for charting their political future.

The first civil war experiences that I underwent in those early years of my life were hard reminders of the life awaiting us children of South Sudan, as we grew up in that volatile political environment. The extreme power exclusion that the people of South Sudan witnessed and brutally experienced from the late 1940s through to the self-rule period (1953–1956) were political developments that generated the seventeen-year civil war, which raged from 1955 to 1972.

I salute all the 1955 fallen heroes for paying the ultimate price for our freedom, and for setting up the nation-state agenda yet to be reached. Their revolutionary legacy will remain with us forever. The 1955 armed revolt in South Sudan marked the beginnings of our liberation struggle, a fact that you, my children and grandchildren, must note.

The SPLA war and other wars over our long struggle against North Sudan's domination of politics are all offspring of the '1955 Torit Army Uprising' – and not the erroneous stories peddled by others that South Sudan's march to freedom started and ended with the SPLA war.

I blossomed to adulthood in the political upheavals of the old Sudan that lasted from 1953 to 2004. I witnessed the emergence of South Sudan as an independent country in 2011, the youngest country in the world that reverted to war with itself in 2013. My generation, and the ones after, have not known lasting peace due to unresolved root causes of our deep internal conflicts, passed on to us by the SPLA war to the present times.

By asking you – our children and the younger generation – to stay connected to the homeland ideals and struggles, all of you will be well positioned in seeking grounds for hope in life while engaging in your development pursuits. This tribute to our fallen heroes is a damning reminder that injustice and oppression in the homeland must be fought through education and development endeavours of the younger generation including their proper growth and contributions to good causes.

We cannot afford to stand aloof in the face of the ongoing brutalities confronting our people. As Elie Wiesel (a holocaust survivor) once said, "Neutrality helps the oppressor, never the victim. Silence encourages the tormentor, never the tormented."

My dear children, your generation should draw strength from experiences of our 1955 heroes to turn around fortunes of our beloved country and must complete the unfinished march to freedom set many decades ago by our iconic leaders.

9

Our Family Roots

I recall conversations I had with my father, Baba Lino Tombe Loku, about my grandfather, Loku Maring Lo'Kitari, on his lifetime journeys that changed the fortunes of his family. Grandpa moved away from Ngulere Village to the Sindiru territory at the end of the nineteenth century, after his first wife and their two offspring passed away. Death, loss, and agony drove my grandfather away from the Lulu'bö territory to Sindiru in the west to avoid revisits of similar family tragedies.

Putting his sad past aside, Grandpa settled well in Sindiru Village – the cradle of the King of the Bari rainmakers, Pitya Lugör – where he raised his three sons: my father, Tombe Loku, Uncle Lodu Loku, and Uncle Wani Loku. Death struck the Lo'Kitari (or Lokitari) family again. My grandmother, Wasuk Na'Mimindya, my father's mother, died – a tragic loss that shook the Loku Lokitari household to the core.

Traumatised by the heartbreaking death of my grandmother, including the past family calamities that faced him back in Ngulere, my grandfather made the difficult decision of moving his three children away from Sindiru Village, further west to Rejaf. That escape from Sindiru was to evade other death misfortunes that my grandfather thought may fall upon his small family.

Grandpa moved his three boys to Rejaf Catholic Mission in search of education for them, a foot journey that took place at the turn of the twentieth century. Traveling one night during the 1923 harvest season in the Sindiru moonlight, my grandfather walked his three sons away from their birth village where their umbilical cords were buried – a no-return journey to Sindiru Village. Carrying his youngest son, Wani, on his shoulders, Grandpa and his two older sons tracked to Rejaf Mission, the final destination of his journey where he remained for good for the sake of the boys' education.

Grandpa never allowed his unfortunate past to torment his future and that of his three children. Although it was, and still is, customary among the Bari people for a man to remarry for the sake of his young children, my grandfather refused to take another wife, fearing that similar death misfortune may revisit his household. He raised his children single-handedly without a mother's support but requested his second son – Uncle Lonjino Lodu Loku – follow a greater calling, that of caring for the family while my father and Uncle Albano Wani Loku went on with their learning at Rejaf Elementary School.

Uncle Lodu's stay away from learning, as demanded by Grandpa, to run the family's chores while his two brothers attended classes was the greatest sacrifice that he made, which the Loku Lokitari's family recognised and hail down the years. It was that family love and stability that Grandpa provided his children, which led to advancement of education of his two sons – my father and Uncle Wani Loku – until they furthered their education thereon.

Years later, my father supported Uncle Lodu Loku to develop his farming livelihood at Pager Village in the Southern Bari chieftaincy of Chief Andrea Gore Umba. Due to that thoughtful arrangement, Uncle Lodu established himself as a good farmer and established our rural home well.

Uncle Lonjino Lodu was a productive farmer and was an anchor figure for the Loku Lokitari's dynasty at Pager Village. Uncle Lodu Loku was an amazing personality that drew the rest of our family to their ancestral and rural roots. To us youngsters in the Lokitari clan, Uncle Lodu made Pager Village an attractive rural home that we proudly visited at the end of every year over the Christmas festive season and during our school vacations.

After settling his family well in the Bari heartlands, my grandfather revived what he loved doing best: carrying out his herbalist practice. Grandpa established himself as a traditional healer specialised in treatment of those affected with guinea worms, the parasitic nematoid worms (*Filaria medinensis*), which back then was an endemic ailment in the land.

Above all, Grandpa saw his first son – my father, Tombe Loku Lokitari – off to his further schooling at Okaru Intermediate School, where Dad schooled there from 1930 to 1934. Three decades later, I followed the same education footsteps that my father set at Okaru, where I learned from 1957 to 1960.

While our children followed the same education trend envisioned by their great-grandfather, I appeal to them to stay connected to our family and ancestral roots while pursuing their education and career dreams – a learning legacy that should be upheld and passed on to our grandchildren. It is that focus and togetherness displayed by the patriarchs of this family which will bond us all to our family values and ancestral roots. I am what I am today because my parents passed on those attributes to me that I religiously uphold up to now – moral norms that should be upheld by the younger generations in the family.

I thank Baba Tombe Loku for setting the education path for us, and for making us all in the family proud of him. Dad told me to get up when I fall down, and to draw lessons from one's failures and stumbles in life to propel oneself to desired goals. Following that mantra, I always got up whenever I fell – defeats that prepared me to know who I am, and which made me stronger in confronting my life's hurdles.

I was taught at home to respect my parents, elders, and members of our family, and never to look down on others, particularly the disadvantaged. My father told us to ignore those who throw slurs at us behind our backs, because, as he said, 'Insults do not grow like trees on one's back'. The Bari version of that saying is, *Tomoresi ti 'durjö ko ŋutu i ki'diŋ gwoso kaden.*

In addition, I was brought up to stay away from harbouring bitterness against others, because preoccupying oneself in indignation is extremely disabling. Through that upbringing approach, I was also raised to stand firm for my rights and the rights of others, and to contribute to good causes.

To my beloved father, I say: Dad, you were an inspiration to the entire Tombe clan. You left an enduring legacy adhered to and honoured by the entire family to this day. We love you and the patriarchs/matriarchs of this family to eternity.

10

Be Proud of Your Names and Roots

Blessed with the beautiful and lovely children that you are, I am sure you all will continue to uphold the family legacy. Although you are negatively impacted by the devastating past and the ongoing internal strife in South Sudan, your resilience in coping with those uncertainties is recognised. It is that positive outlook in life that will keep you anchored to your ancestral and African roots. That untampered sense of belonging and purpose will greatly help you all journey to your desired goals.

Prepare yourselves to contribute more towards advancement and development of your children, our grandchildren – developed human potential and expertise that will be needed in post-war rebuilding of South Sudan and the African continent when the time comes. Mother Africa is waiting for you to respond to that calling. Your commitment to stay on course for attainment of these noble goals will be hailed and applauded all. I am proud you are sailing to that end.

My dear children, the raging war in South Sudan has devastated you, shattered the lives of our people, and totally ruined the education of your generation. Millions of our youths, including you, were/are forced into exile in far lands. The internally displaced populations in the country are brutally suppressed and are faced with the stark reality of living in inhuman conditions and environments. You and our grandchildren together are products of that immeasurable and devastating human dispersal – all caused by the ruinous wars in the country. You are, sadly, sucked into that instability cycle and chaos that must be got rid of.

Despite all the hardships you are facing, you are providing your children with the best education you can afford. We are proud of you in availing them education and development opportunities in these challenging times. Above all of this, I applaud you all for making yourselves and our grandchildren proud of their names and roots.

Cultivating your children's awareness of where they come from is critical for their proper growth, which is a major step towards bringing more meaning to their lives. That sense of belonging to the family, the community, and the society at large must be reinforced through parental support and direction, which gladly you are providing.

In keeping you and your children connected to the Tombe family, you are already adhering to our ancestral roots, and are availing our grandchildren with the opportunity to complete their backgrounds. That sense of belonging is a crucial anchor for them to overcome the challenges they face in a harsh world in which their race is oftentimes marginalised and brutally looked down upon.

Providing them with the proper tools and moral norms is a must. Empower them to navigate their lives with utmost care against the backdrop of the devastating racial profiling happening on a daily basis in the far lands.

You and our grandchildren are valued for who you are and whom you relate to – strong ties brought about by your closeness to the family, community, and society at large. That family bond reinforces your children's sense of self-worth, honesty, and sincerity – essential values that will prepare them to aim higher in life and to value others. Imbibing these principles in your children is the greatest contribution you will have made to ready them to live well in this unstable world.

Assist your loved ones to live with meaning and purpose while pursuing their educational dreams, and support them all along to develop a positive outlook in life. Brought up in this way, your offspring will have been prepared well for passing on compelling ideas for promotion of the greater good.

In the present world, where single stories are frequently pedalled about minorities, you must groom your children to tell their own stories to cancel the single negative narratives told about them by others. Their strong sense of belonging to your roots will greatly help them to overcome their fears. Provide your youngsters with the required knowledge to enable them to tell their own stories.

In that way, you will have made your children well-grounded socially, culturally, and in good stead for the future. That's the power of storytelling in which the bad is redeemed by the good. Let our grandchildren benefit from the African proverb which says, 'As long as a lion doesn't convey its own story, it's the hunter's tales that will be talked about – not the bravery of the lion'.

Guard against telling yourselves and your loved ones that life is hard and not worth living. Such belittling of yourselves is bound to send devastating ripples across one's remaining life and that of your children. Let you and our grandchildren say, "I am strong, I am beautiful, I am intelligent; and I am a change-maker that will better myself, my family, and the greater community."

Let you and our grandchildren change any past sad stories – if there are any – to that of hope for a promising future. Turn any misfortunes that you faced in the past, and which may still be confronting you to the present day, to positive drives for bringing more meaning to your lives and that of your children.

My beloved children, for those of you living in far lands away from the motherland, prepare yourselves and our grandchildren for a return to our continent when the time comes, as the African renaissance is in the horizon.

As your children may stay away in the 'West' or elsewhere in the world, for the most part of their lives, much longer than expected – with some of them probably opting to live away from the homeland permanently – you should from now onward prepare them well to face the blatant realities of life in the diaspora.

Let them stay connected to the family while inculcating in them the African way of life through organised visits to safer parts of the African continent. Such linkages to Mother Africa will essentially keep them abreast with the current doings and transformations happening in our continent. All of you should tap into those ever-changing developments in Africa. The knowledge that you and your loved ones will acquire on such visits will enrich all of you culturally and intellectually.

Your guidance and console are critically needed for proper upbringing of our grandchildren as responsible citizens wherever they are on this our planet. And all along, you must teach them to prepare themselves to live meaningfully and safely in an ever-changing and challenging world.

11

Parenting is Forever

Whatever I did and continue to do in life, I am always energised by my parents – long gone to the afterlife – and more so by you, my beloved children and family.

Although I vowed in the past never to expose you to the horrors of armed conflicts and social upheavals, those bygone promises were not fulfilled due to a number of factors: the instability and anarchy that prevailed back then in the 'Old Sudan', and the total disorder faced to the present day in South Sudan.

Our headache, to date, is in the parental failure not to have settled all of you in a stable and peaceful environment for the realisation of your full potential. For most of your young lives, you spent crucial growth years running away from harm. Those were matters and events that were beyond us all; the protracted past conflicts in the undivided Sudan, and the anarchism raging in South Sudan to the present day. All along, it was our utmost duty to shield and keep you away from any harm that we judged would have retarded your proper growth and educational development.

Although now in your adulthood, you have not probably got the full grasp and understanding of the confusions of protracted conflicts, and the human dispersal associated with horrors of war that immensely devastated our people in the motherland – turmoil that shattered hopes and dreams of survivors.

For those of you currently living in the 'West' with your children, you have so far done well in the face of life's adversities. However, your siblings and next of kin struggling in different parts of the African continent – who are worse off than can be imagined – are facing more hardships and the gravest conditions. We pray that they pull through those tough times.

The wrought of misfortunes burdening a few of you – living abroad or in the motherland – are heart-rending developments that we, your parents, have not come to terms with up to now. At trying times of your lives, we have always reassured you all along that all is not lost. Young as you are, there are vast opportunities out there waiting for your taking. Tap into the vast potential, energy, and creativity ingrained in you for turning around your fortunes.

Over the years, we were fully aware of our parental responsibilities that we fulfilled, although those obligations have now dwindled in these our sundown years. However, since parenting is forever, there is that part of us still waiting to be exploited by you for the benefit of you, our lovely children. Stay connected. Come, let's share thoughts and ideas together that will open doors for you.

Overall, we at home recognise your unflinching determination to succeed. Although there were twists and turns in your growth and education journeys, you overcame those personal development challenges by working hard to reach your accomplished goals. You attained those personal development objectives with flying colours and are now settled down to your careers and professions. We profoundly thank you for reaching those skies.

Bearing in mind the established parenting ways, I encourage you all, as the saying goes, to 'do unto yourselves and your children as you wish your parents had done unto you.' 'No matter how far we come, our parents are always in us.' Doing right is an obligation that must be fulfilled to our last breaths. Draw this monumental inspiration for betterment of yourselves and your own families, and for contributing towards good causes despite the hurdles faced.

I thank you all, my beloved children, for riding the storms over the high seas to the calmer shores; for keeping yourselves focused on whatever you do in life throughout until now; and for raising your children, our grandchildren, well. And thank you very much for your huge contributions towards improvement of our lives and wellness. We are what we are today because of your unquestionable support. You are loved immensely to infinity.

12

Away to Boarding School

My Dear Children,

I went away to boarding school, and that moving away from home was, in a sense, my initiation to adulthood. My first adventure to the outside world – an opening that dramatically changed my life from then onward.

On the upbringing front, I went away from the preying eyes of my strict parents, who became more controlling as I matured, but was more armed with our home and cultural values to face the outside world. Although I was liberated from parental control, I was very grateful to my parents for the strong upbringing that readied me to face the outside world. I looked forward to what I imagined would be a transformational life, which amazingly unfolded while I was away learning at Okaru.

Why am I telling you all these, my dear children? I am doing so because you should know the story of my life starting from those childhood beginnings, narrated for your appreciation of my early struggles. The strict upbringing at home made me acquire mental toughness, and character building accumulated at those early stages of my growth – nothing like it that which, my children, experienced during your early childhood and juvenile years. It is also a story about peer competition that led to achievement of excellence in our days, anchored on the mantra that 'what you can do, I can do it better'.

Moving on with my education years later, I had the opportunity of thanking my parents, particularly my stepmom, Mama Anyeze Kiteŋ, for the rewarding upbringing they accorded me during my tender years. Those child-rearing ways cultivated my focus in whatever I did and still do to this day – home-education norms that moulded me to the person I am today.

I completed my primary-level learning successfully at Kator Elementary School in 1956, gaining admission to Okaru Intermediate School for the 1957 school year. At the onset of my classroom learning to the very end of my junior-school journey, my father was pleased with my focus in schooling. He was extremely pleased that I followed his footsteps in getting education at Okaru Intermediate School, where he schooled from 1930 to 1934. I joined Okaru Sacred Heart School in 1957, more than two decades after my father left.

After the establishment of the minor seminary at Okaru, the religious centre gradually grew into a learning complex, with start of the intermediate school section. Both founded at Rejaf Catholic Mission in 1927, the two schools were moved to Okaru in 1928 and 1929 respectively. The junior school section was formally inaugurated in July 1932, through celebration of a Pontifical High Mass in which the school was named 'Okaru Sacred Heart Intermediate School'.

While Okaru with its cool weather was well suited for learning, the Intermediate School became a renowned learning institution through the years. It positioned itself as a solid foundation for the promotion of junior education in the South back then, along with the few intermediate schools established in other parts of Southern Sudan.

Okaru Intermediate School became a beacon for the consolidation of the moral values that we acquired at home. The aggregate of the learning standards we got at Sacred Heart School, and the value norms garnered at home, were together the ideals that prepared me well for further education – values that equally readied me to face the world outside the classroom.

Pursuance of our education in that respect was considered by our educators as crucial for consolidation of our mental growth, personal development, and deemed essential to ready us for development of our country.

At Okaru, our teachers also mentored us to recognise the value of voice in society and cultivated our awareness on the danger of double standards. Through that mentoring, we incrementally gained knowledge on the principles of rights and wrongs, and a little bit of know-how on promotion of the right of citizens to struggle for their freedom and good causes. Those core values formed the ideals that prepared us to face the harsh world, and which made us God-fearing citizens.

Armed with those learning and upbringing principles, I oftentimes return to those mantras in conducting my life, particularly when dealing with demanding situations. Although our out-of-class experiences at Okaru Intermediate School were a rude awakening to the political realities of the old Sudan, that education path prepared us well, to a certain degree, to face the political upheavals at the time.

In preparing us to concentrate on our learning in that unsettling political environment in the Sudan, our learning mentors warned us that the 'Southern Problem' was a protracted political conflict against the Northern Sudanese oppression of the people of South Sudan – a liberation struggle that needed cool heads to deal with.

In that respect, our teachers emphasised that our role in the Southern Sudan freedom struggle required us – the younger generation at the time – to continue with our education as a contribution towards the long march to freedom.

It was that development approach which my generation followed through the attainment of their education over those conflict years. We never disappointed our parents and learning mentors by accomplishing those set learning goals thereon.

13

The Groundswell Calling

After Okaru, I embarked on my secondary-school journey fully aware of the political storms that awaited us – the 1955 army uprising that I got glimpses of which was a hard reminder of the life ahead of us children of South Sudan back then.

Before I joined Rumbek, the Sudan was already at the verge of another civil war, five years after the first civil war in the country broke out in Torit Town on 18 August 1955. Our political leaders fled en masse to East and Central Africa at the end of 1960, escaping into exile that took place for purposes of launching the freedom struggle. That national self-determination drive stemmed out of the total control of power by the rulers in Khartoum, which resulted in ruthless repression of the people of South Sudan and enforcement of the Arabisation programme in the South.

I recall the extraordinary natural occurrences in Southern Sudan in 1960, viewed at the time as signs of the wrath of the gods against the evils about to befall the homeland. We witnessed nature's roars over that period – the rumblings of lightning and thunder accompanied by relentless long rains that caused unprecedented floods during the 1960 rainy season.

Those heavenly warnings started with the Nile River

floods in which many parts of Juba City and other parts of Southern Sudan along the river basin were inundated. While the famous 'Konyokonyo Market' in Juba Town and other parts of the urban landscape along the Nile were entirely submerged in the floodwaters, millions of the population living downstream were uprooted from their homes and localities.

I vividly remember the 1960 and 1961 earthquakes that shook Juba Town, tremors that terrified the populations in the urban sprawl. Those earthquakes were considered as attributes of the 'Rejaf Mountain' by the Bari people; the tremors were/are part of the East African Rift System (EARS) that causes interaction of three tectonic plates: the Nubian, the Somalian, and the Arabian formations. Geologically, the divergent tectonic plate boundary, with its movement affecting the Lake Victoria region, extends to Burundi, Rwanda, Zambia, Tanzania, Malawi, Mozambique, Congo DR, Uganda, and South Sudan.

Three decades ago in 1990, a 7.2 magnitude earthquake struck southeast of Juba City – the strongest tremor recorded in South Sudan in the past 123 years after the heaviest quakes that measured M6+, which occurred in 1900. South Sudan is located within the East African earthquake region, which is why that part of the country is prone to quakes.

During the 1960s tremors, unexplained incidences occurred. Rats were sent out of their holes and quarters, running all over town on account of the earth shocks. Watching the rodents dashing about in panic was a worrying scene that shook the citizens in town out of their wits – particularly young children that were petrified by those rare natural occurrences. I witnessed those frightening incidences.

According to legendary predictions of the Bari people, those were nature's warnings. The unprecedented floods and the earthquakes that daunted Southern Sudan in the 1960s were signs of bad omen over the motherland. The natural disasters were taken by the indigenous populations as telling signs of the looming north-south armed conflict that erupted in August 1955 – a vicious war that lasted for seventeen years, from 1955 to 1972, which resulted in untold human loss that reduced Southern Sudan to wasteland.

I joined Rumbek Secondary School in 1961 in the midst of that worrying and chaotic political environment, knowing very well that a devastating war was in the offing. Nevertheless, we were determined to get on with our education despite the looming dangers ahead of us.

Learning at Rumbek and in the other education institutions was retarded by the worsening political instability in South Sudan back then. Students at the school went on strike that led to closure of classes in September 1962. The chaotic situation at the school led to dispatch of the students to their respective locations and regions.

The knock-on effect of that Rumbek School standoff mushroomed into widespread schools' strikes across Southern Sudan up to the primary-school level. A the end of 1962, the education system in the South was brought to a halt by those schoolchildren strikes.

The school remonstrations generated the groundswell running away of students to the neighbouring countries. The relentless escape of the schoolchildren from Southern Sudan to exile steadily gathered momentum towards the end of 1962, with the flight of schoolboys to Uganda, Congo, Kenya, and Tanzania that drew the attention of the international community to the political crisis in the Sudan. That unstoppable escape of schoolchildren to East and Central Africa continued through to the 1970s and beyond.

Back to the 1950s and 1960s, Rumbek and Juba Commercial Secondary Schools were the only secondary schools that catered for higher learning in South Sudan back then. The two schools played pivotal roles in the liberation politics of South Sudan at the time. In the absence of institutional infrastructures in the South then, Rumbek and Juba Commercial Secondary Schools also served as political platforms for consolidation and relaunch of our freedom struggle.

To that end, the two schools served as 'melting pot' conclaves for enhancement of the political struggle against Northern Sudan's extreme misrule. To that effect, Rumbek and Juba Commercial secondary schools played a major role in grooming our political leaders, with Rumbek in particular playing lead role in that political drive since the founding of the school in 1948.

From those early liberation struggles till I joined Rumbek in 1961, the school served as a political hub for the promotion of the freedom movement, particularly at the height of the political tensions in the 1950s to 1960s, through to the 1970s. Secondary-school students and lower-level schoolchildren across Southern Sudan back then played a pivotal role in revival of the region's political consciousness against repression of blacks in the Sudan.

Behind the scenes, Rumbek Secondary School played a major role in mobilisation of that groundswell momentum – a political awakening that triggered the students' exodus into exile that subsequently led to a relaunch of the armed struggle in South Sudan in November 1962 – the second phase of the first civil war in Sudan that ended in attainment of partial peace in March 1972. My generation contributed heavily to those liberation ideals, and remained loyal to that freedom call to the end while they followed their education goals.

14

Escape to Exile

I escaped to Uganda at the end of September 1962 without telling my parents about that life-changing departure from home to an unknown destination and future. That flight to East Africa was an outcome of the school strikes that rocked the education institutions across Southern Sudan in 1960 through to 1962 – learning instability caused by the political turmoil in the country.

I was in the first group of Rumbek students that left the country to join the 'Southern Sudan Liberation Movement' (SSLM), founded in exile for the relaunch of our freedom struggle – the escape to East Africa that ended our education in Sudan. On that flight trail, we travelled to Parajok, a small border town in Eastern Equatoria where we fled through the bushes of the Acholi territory to Kitgum Town in Uganda.

Alerted about our escape, the Sudanese security forces stationed at the border town of Parajok took immediate action to arrest us, an apprehension plan that we uncovered in the nick of time. We slipped out of Parajok in haste to avert the arrest – a runaway to the Uganda-Sudan border that was a combination of hard walk and run through the Acholi countryside.

We safely crossed to Uganda after a gruesome foot journey through the harsh bushes and forests. A day after, we arrived in Kitgum Town on the morning of 9 October 1962, to a fanfare of Uganda's first independence anniversary – celebrations that included an official public rally, an armed forces parade, and a display of traditional dances. That was my first encounter with the free world, an East African country that had just freed itself from decades of British colonial bondage.

Those independence celebrations were life's experiences freshly embedded in my mind to date. The festivities showed me, in real terms, what freedom and liberty meant to mankind. Young as we were, that independence anniversary was a huge motivator for our freedom mission. Witnessing that *uhuru* (freedom) festival was an amazing way of starting off our liberation journey.

The first refugee students to arrive in Uganda on its independence centennial, we were also the first batch of students from Southern Sudan to reach Kampala City at the end of October 1962. Hardly a week later, bands of schoolchildren from South Sudan streaked to the Ugandan capital – a flight of youngsters to Uganda that alarmed authorities of Prime Minister Milton Obote's administration.

Unrecognised as refugees in Uganda initially, we received no support from the government. Humanitarian organisations were non-existent at the time for us to run to for charitable support. In the absence of aid assistance, our hardships mounted, which rolled on for many years thereon. We turned for support to the small South Sudanese communities domiciled in Uganda's major towns and cities. Thankfully, they obliged.

Our communities in Kampala and in the other parts of Uganda dealt with the students' influx to the country by accommodating many youths in their houses, huge support that came our way when we were in dire need of shelter and food.

A group of us were accommodated by Hon Ibrahim Nyigilo – a well-known ex-soldier of the No. 2 Battalion forced into exile after the 1955 Torit military uprising. Squeezing ourselves in the available rest spaces in Ibrahim's small cottage at nightfall proved a nightmare for us and our hosts.

In her ingenious ways, Madam Nyigillo found a solution to overcome our sleeping problem by turning her small kitchen, every single night, into a sleeping area for us. That arrangement was made possible through removal of kitchen hardware and food items before we retired for the night in that small room. Those drills continued throughout our stay at Ibrahim Nyigilo's residence.

Accommodating over ten students in a house meant for a small family was extremely strenuous, but Madam Nyigilo braved the task to the end by carrying out those chores with utmost motherly care and love that I fondly remember to this very day.

Once retired to our sleeping quarters, meticulous drills had to be made by us to make our sleep in that small space every night as comfortable as possible. We packed ourselves like sardines into that limited sleeping area through a well-rehearsed programme followed to the letter.

Once settled for the night, on the cold cement floor, each member in the sleeping party was sternly warned by the group leaders against unnecessary turns and twists during sleep; and were seriously cautioned to keep nature calls to bare minimum at night, as sleep patterns would be dislodged by such wakeups. Anyone fond of throwing himself about during sleep under those difficult sleeping conditions was also seriously warned and rebuked to shed off those bad habits. We told ourselves, through hard jokes, to desist from revisiting the comfortable life we were once so accustomed of back home in Southern Sudan.

Preparing for our sleep every single night over our stay at the Nakawa residential estate was a painful feat that we faced till we left Ibrahim Nyigillo's house.

That was how we lived at the Nakawa Residential Estate till we left for Southern Sudan to participate in the relaunch of the armed struggle that took place in November 1962. Years later, I looked up Hon Ibrahim Nyigillo in Juba just to thank him for the huge and unforgettable support that he and his dear wife accorded us while we stayed in his house back in 1962.

At the political level, Hon Ibrahim's massive contributions to the liberation movement were unsung by the state and leaders of South Sudan. Let me take the opportunity in this letter to recognise Hon Ibrahim Nyigillo for his invaluable contributions to the liberation cause. Although ignored, like the other unsung heroes of South Sudan, Hon Nyigillo's contributions are nonetheless recorded in the annals of our history. His name and that of the other Torit uprising heroes will be remembered forever.

After we left the Nakawa Estate, our lives took a tumble for the worst. Our accommodation and feeding needs were not addressed by the Ugandan authorities. We struggled on our own for months on end. We pulled through by God's grace, and through sheer determination to live.

On the liberation front, we discovered that our political

leaders in exile back then were not ready for relaunch of the armed struggle. They were unready politically and financially to undertake that huge liberation task – a state of unpreparedness that was heartbreaking to all the movement stalwarts, and to the people of South Sudan.

To us students in exile, that unreadiness for the drive of the liberation struggle was shocking, as it was contrary to the groundswell mobilisation undertaken by the Southern Sudan Liberation Movement (SSLM) leaders.

Despite the political flaws in the relaunch of the armed struggle as planned, the actual recruitment to the rebel army picked up pace at the height of the students' exodus to East Africa. That revolutionary momentum subsequently led to the widespread conscription of the 1955 ex-fighters – settled in Uganda as refugees – to the initial rebel force that kicked off the armed struggle on 16 November 1962.

Although the armed struggle against North Sudan was initially launched as a conventional war, the military leaders changed that strategy by embarking on a protracted guerrilla warfare, a decision taken amidst the backdrop of the SSLM unreadiness for a frontal war against the Northern Sudanese army.

Involvement of minors in a guerrilla war, in the view of our military leaders, was a waste of South Sudan's human potential that would be needed for the future rebuilding of the country. On account of that military standpoint, all the youngsters who joined the bush war were dismissed forthwith from the liberation army. We, the students already recruited to the initial rebel force, protested against those discharge orders.

Clinging to the earlier nuances and calls for the minors to participate in the bush war as originally planned by the political leaders, we students insisted and pressed for our participation in the liberation force. In our appeals against that military decree, we begged for the reversal of our dismissal from the rebel force. We pointedly made references to the groundswell campaign that we students at Rumbek School worked so hard for relaunch of the first civil war in Sudan that eventually was triggered by the schoolboys' exodus to East Africa.

Those students' demands were overruled by the top rebel commanders. They stood their ground by ordering us out of the military camps, and emphatically told us to go away for the advancement of our education. The schoolchildren contribution to the liberation struggle, according to the military leaders, was not in the war front, but rather in readying themselves educationally for the post-war development of South Sudan.

In compliance with those military orders, all the youngsters moved out of the military camps. We fled back to Uganda, Kenya, and Tanzania in earnest, in search of schooling. That's how the back-to-school campaign of Southern Sudan's school-going children in exile was generated, which subsequently led to our extensive education in exile.

On the execution of that education plan, my close friends and I moved to Arua in North-western Uganda, where most of the refugee students were temporarily settled. That move to Uganda's West Nile Region was an initial start of our education journey in East Africa.

Hon Phillip Yengkeji, a renowned schoolteacher and a well-known politician hailing from Southern Bari, like my father, invited me and a few of my companions to stay at his residence. As a close friend of my father, Hon Yengkeji couldn't allow me to stay in one of the temporary refugee settlements in Arua Town other than his home.

Events turned for the worst for the refugee students in Uganda. Rumours circulating in Arua Town had it that the Ugandan authorities were planning to deport the Sudanese refugee students back to Southern Sudan. Those deportation gossips were purportedly based on Uganda's Interior Minister Felix Onama's insistence that the refugee students should be returned to Sudan, as requested by the authorities in Khartoum.

Our peers, settled in one of the unused schools in Arua Town, ran amok one morning on learning about those deportation orders. In the pandemonium that followed, the panic-stricken refugee students swiftly ran away from Arua, and headed towards the Zaire (now DRC Congo) borders. The rest of the refugee youngsters living in various parts of Arua Municipality, including myself, joined the fleeing party.

Running hard for our lives away to the Congo-Uganda border, we reached Nderi early evening of that day. Nderi was a border hamlet in Zaire, about ten to fifteen kilometres away from Uganda's Arua Town. Our sudden arrival at Nderi Village, while panting for our breath after the long run, almost caused more panic and mayhem within the local community in that small Congo town.

The village chief, a cool-headed local authority, welcomed us to his administrative area and immediately accommodated us in a deserted school. The school building, with its zinc roof still intact, was stripped bare to its brickworks by the elements over years of extreme neglect on account of the 1960s civil war in Zaire.

Having ridden the deportation storms to safety in Nderi Hamlet, we were extremely grateful to our hosts for their hospitality. The hardships that set in hit us hard after a few days on that Christmas week. The livelihood hurdles that we faced included lack of water, inadequate food supplies, rough sleeping conditions, and acute shortage of medical care. In the African spirit of welcoming people facing the extremities of conflict, the local authorities at Nderi routinely marshalled edibles for us from the local farmers.

A few days later, the situation at the temporary refugee settlement grew unbearable with arrival of new refugee students – streaming into the little town on daily basis, all of them accommodated in the school refugee camp. Under those deteriorating conditions, we literally kept our cool and sanity through survival and determination.

The community chief eventually succeeded, after many attempts, to have us moved out of Nderi Village to Aru Town – a small border town in Zaire's Ituri District, Oriental Province, located closer to Arua town in Uganda.

The actual evacuation journey to Aru took place on Christmas Day 1962 – the first Christmas ever that we spent away from our homes. The truck that transported us to Aru town rumbled on, making rasping sounds as it navigated its way on the rough road and difficult terrain.

Gripped by a dizzying sense of insecurity as the lorry roared on, I wasn't sure where we were heading to. Anyway, my thoughts rolled back to the usual festive indulgences back home that adorned the Christmas celebrations, and how strange we were caught up in a difficult road journey to an unknown destination on that Christmas day.

Those thoughts preoccupied my mind as the truck sped away to Aru Town. Arriving at our destination late on that Christmas evening, we were hurriedly camped in an old and unused Church building, along the main road opposite a *gendarmerie* (soldiers) unit. The soldiers at that small military location were stationed across the road opposite our new refugee camp. They proudly carried their weapons around with their fingers on the triggers – giving us the frightening impression that they were ready to shoot anyone around the vicinity on the slightest provocation.

That unused Church became our home for the next five months. The hardships of refugee life set in, which grew harder by the day: the improper feeding arrangements; the 'night blindness' that gripped us a few months after; the unhygienic living conditions faced; and the uncertainties about our future in Zaire (DR Congo) that worried us much. We faced those untenable conditions because we were unrecognised as refugees in Zaire.

There was no one to turn to for any support at that initial stage of our stay at Aru. Even the governor of Oriental Province who visited the refugee camp during our long stay there told us that the government of Zaire was unable to meet our needs. With no government or aid agencies' support forthcoming, we were left on our own, except for the limited food items that trickled in from the local farmers – mobilised from time to time by the local chief for provision of life-saving rations to us.

Towards the end of the first quarter of 1963, many of our colleagues left the Aru refugee settlement for Uganda in search of education. Without financial resources for funding our travel to Uganda to try our luck in search of schooling, many of us were stuck at the refugee camp, with nobody to turn to for financial help for facilitation of our trip to East Africa.

15

Risky Visit Home

Unable to raise the required cash locally in Congo for the facilitation of our education adventures in East Africa, a close friend and I ventured back to Yei and Juba to fetch whatever little financial support our parents could garner for us for that purpose. Considering that we were already branded enemies of Sudan by the Khartoum government back then, that return home – to Yei and Juba – was an extremely risky journey to conjure and embark on, but one that we undertook for getting the required funds for search of our schooling in Uganda.

The foot journey from the Aru refugee settlement to Yei was the easiest part of our long venture back to South Sudan. We arrived in Yei Town in early February 1963 and stayed in my friend's house undercover for three days before we proceeded to Juba. Setting off for the eastbound journey on bicycles at 4:00am on Friday 8 February 1963, we reached Juba city safely at sunset on the same day – a gruelling journey accomplished without security complications.

Although the one-hundred-mile Juba-Yei highway was constantly patrolled by the Sudan Armed Forces (SAF) in search of the Anya-Nya rebels back then, luckily, on that day, our trip on that motorway was free of military patrols. After a brief rest at the foot of Körök Mountain (AKA *Jebel Kujur* in colloquial Arabic) – a few miles away from our home – we entered the city at dusk.

Everyone in the family was utterly shocked when I turned up at the family home at the Kator residential sprawl. Although my father was exceedingly shocked at my sudden reappearance at home under those worrying security conditions, he was, on the flip side, relieved to see me alive after a long separation. Nevertheless, my dad was overly furious at our adventure to very unsafe Southern Sudan – stating that our venture to Juba under those intolerable and dangerous conditions was totally reckless. However, he welcomed my homecoming with a family prayer.

Worried about our safety, my father ordered us to stay for a short period to avoid arrest incidences – directives that we strictly adhered to. We left Juba after a week's stay. Before our return journey to Zaire (the DR Congo), our families generously raised the funds we requested for financing our trip to Uganda in search of schooling. We were back in Yei at the end of third week in February 1963.

After a brief stopover in Yei, we returned safely to our refugee settlement in Zaire – arriving at our final destination to a deserted refugee settlement. Many students had already left the church refugee camp at Aru for Uganda. The few of our colleagues left behind at the refugee camp were on the verge of leaving Congo for the education adventures in East Africa.

All of us were drawn to East Africa, particularly to Uganda, on account of the favourable policy changes towards refugee education there. The churches in Uganda raised funds through their charity organisations for schooling of Sudanese refugees in the country – learning opportunities that our colleagues benefited from, including myself.

A month after my departure to Kampala, I gained admission at St Mary's College Kisubi – thanks to Stanslaus Awad Tombe, my childhood friend and classmate at Okaru and Rumbek. Stans Awad played a major role in my admission to Kisubi and was also instrumental in enrolment of other refugee students to St Mary's College.

Given Awad's past exceptional academic records that he presented to gain a place at St Mary's, in addition to his outstanding academic performance at the school, those exceptional learning credentials were the leverage that influenced the headmaster to take more Sudanese refugee students to learn at Kisubi. In addition to prowess of the South Sudanese students in sports and other extra curricula activities, St Mary's headteacher – Brother Paul Bourges – was exceedingly willing in enrolling more Southern Sudanese students to learn at the college over the years. Stanslaus Awad Tombe was the influencer and magnet for drawing many of us South Sudanese students to St Mary's College.

Going back to school after a long break from learning was the best thing that happened to me, as I had already lost hope in furthering my education in exile. I schooled at St Mary's until I completed my A level studies in 1967. My years at Kisubi were overall eventful and successful in all aspects of education.

I joined Makerere University in July 1968, fully equipped with life's values and precepts, and was ready to face the world ahead of me with confidence, having drawn so much from my school experiences, both in South Sudan and in Uganda.

On graduating from Makerere in March 1972, I secured a teaching job in Matongo Secondary School in Sondu, Kisii Province – located fifty-seven miles away from Kisumu on the Kisumu-Kisii highway.

I left my teaching post after one year, upon getting disturbing news from the family back in Juba that my father was seriously ill, a worrying situation that required my presence in Juba as an elder son in the family. The family urged for my immediate return to the Sudan, an abrupt departure back home that shortened my teaching contract at Matongo Secondary School. With that abrupt return to Sudan, I also suspended my further studies plans.

I returned to Juba in March 1973 after eleven years in exile. That homecoming and family reunion was tearful, accompanied with moving outbursts. My father looked frail and was evidently sick but was in high spirits in welcoming me back home. My brothers, sisters, cousins/nieces, and the rest of the relatives looked worn out through years of strife and hard lives. Although the family get-together was emotional, it was nevertheless joyous and celebratory. That's how my family warmly welcomed me back home after years of separation.

From that point on, I realised the responsibilities that awaited my intervention for the improvement of livelihoods of the Tombe family – enormous responsibilities awaiting tackling that frightened me to the core. I was totally floored and loaded with worries about my father's poor health, how I would support our family, and how to confront the uncertainties of life that awaited me.

I delivered on those responsibilities through sheer determination and unyielding resolve. I sponsored my siblings' education, including some of my cousins'/nieces' schooling, and took care of our family household needs; and above all, I addressed my father's health and well-being needs. I managed all that before I established my own family and raised our children.

16

Welcome Home, Anytime, All the Time

My Beloved Children,

When I left home for exile in 1962, I did so without saying goodbye to my parents. I didn't tell them the intentions of my flight to East Africa, which was to participate in the freedom struggle, a runaway that was shrouded in secrecy in keeping with the freedom struggle codes back then.

Our family, particularly my father, was deeply worried about my unexpected and unannounced departure from home to unchartered waters. Five months later, I returned to South Sudan from Congo, where I was temporally settled as a refugee. That return home was my last appearance in Juba prior to my long stay away from the motherland, which ended in mid-1973.

On that risky return home to Juba, I was availed the opportunity to make amends with my parents for leaving Southern Sudan in the previous year without obtaining their permission and blessings. Like a 'prodigal son', I begged my father for forgiveness, which he gladly granted.

On that homecoming in February 1963, I stayed for one week having quality time, holding hands with family members, sharing love, and reminiscing about our good old days. On leaving the family after that brief home visit, my dad approved my departure back to Zaire – a second departure to exile approved and blessed by the family. That time round, I was extremely happy to have left home assured of my parents' permission and love.

After the family send-off prayers were concluded, before my return to Congo, my father said, "Son, I know you are quite strong to survive out there on your own. Be the best that you always are. Our awesome God and ancestors will guide every step you make while you are far away from home in strange lands. Remember to keep and use our traditional values and moral norms as your guiding principles in whatever you do out there. Go and experience the world, son, and come back to us stronger and wiser."

Walking away from home that early morning at the start of the long and difficult return to Congo, my father's words of wisdom rang in my mind while I journeyed on to the hardships that awaited us at our refugee destination. Throughout that trip, memories over memories about my early childhood rolled back. I vividly recalled the rigidly structured life carved out for us children by our parents as we grew up – eventful juvenile years full of home education and children's activities. Missing the good life and home comfort, I appreciated how lucky I was to have been brought up well by my loving family.

While travelling through the beautiful Central Equatoria terrain on that long trip to Zaire, my thoughts were transfixed on our tender years at Hai Neem residential block in Juba Town. I thought of our active and vibrant life back then, one that was full of adventures which every child on the block desired. Reflections rolled back on our play activities that consisted of ball games, building of toy cars made of straws and reeds, hide-and-seek playoffs conducted in the Neem hedges around the house perimeters, and memories of many more pastimes that we conjured.

In the course of that foot journey in the wild to Congo, I vividly recalled the ball games we played on the hard grounds full of protruding pebbles that injured every player. I sneakily smiled, marvelling on those times while we trekked in the dense bushes and forests – reflecting on our limping home after those games back at Hai Neem and pretending that we were okay despite the foot injuries sustained. Peer pressure made each one of us hold our tears back to prove our machismo, although the throbbing pains in our feet were unbearable.

Those thoughts about our eventful childhood years kept rolling back in my mind as I travelled to my exile destination. I recalled the small balls that we made out of wrapped-around rags, used as footballs played on those brutal playgrounds – feats that were not meant for the faint-hearted. Playing ball games on those hard surfaces was, in a way, proof of our hardiness to demanding situations. I look back to those play activities as character-building undertakings, childhood adventures, and toughness that I miss to this very day.

As I travelled through the Yei District countryside to Congo, my thoughts also wondered back to the 1950s and the 1960s, in which children were brought up by parents and the community to be responsible members in the family and society. We were watched over, with any mistakes corrected along as we blossomed. I reminded myself of that tough upbringing and character-building which we endured. I was engrossed in those childhood reflections till I reached my destination. Summation of all those childhood happenings earned me the mental toughness that helped me greatly in dealing with demanding refugee life.

Given those infantile experiences, plus the precepts obtained in the learning institutions thereon, I held on to those upbringing dictums in conducting my later life. My generation were forged out of those strict childhood disciplines that prepared us to overcome the challenges that we faced in later life. Prepared well that way, we rode the storms that confronted us in exile and thereafter. Those life's drills groomed me into the adult I am today.

My beloved children, for those of you who left home and are managing your lives while far away from the family, remember you have gone away with our blessings and love. Come home when you can. Children, 'I know you are quite strong to survive out there on your own. Be the best that you always are'. My father told me that when I left home for exile in the early 1960s.

My children, you are welcomed home anytime, all the time, and remember, you are forever loved unconditionally. Lean yourselves on the family pillar, as that togetherness will bring more meaning to your lives and that of our grandchildren. As Maya Angelou – the American memoirist, poet, and civil rights activist – said, 'Make a practice of coming home where love awaits you'.

17

Unfinished Journey to Freedom

Born in South Sudan over seven decades ago, I journeyed through two devasting wars in Sudan that lasted from 1955 to 1972, and from 1983 to 2004. I witnessed the emergence of South Sudan as a sovereign state in July 2011 – a young country founded after the Comprehensive Peace Agreement (CPA) that leaders of South and North Sudan signed in January 2005, and implemented thereon. Nine years after the CPA, the third war in South Sudan erupted on 15 December 2013 – a vicious internal strife tearing our young country apart to the present day. Simply put, I am a product of three prolonged wars.

The devastating consequences of the three protracted wars caused unprecedented human dispersal that reduced the country to ground zero, and which created a long-running refugee problem haunting South Sudan to the present day. Never in my wildest imaginations have I ever thought our young country would revert back to a home-generated war that reduced the homeland to its present lowest level.

South Sudan is brought down by the current political leaders in power, the very people who struggled in the past against oppression, inequality, and injustice – thus worsening the very backwardness that the people of South Sudan fought hard to eliminate. In driving the current war, the current rulers turned their backs to the promotion of peace and the rebuilding of the young nation. They brushed aside and trivialised the sacrifices of our heroes and heroines who paid the ultimate price for our freedom. Rubbishing that martyrdom is travesty of the sovereignty gained.

The raging internal strife is caused by staggering leadership failures, namely: extreme misrule that led to demolition of the rule of law, total capture of the national wealth for promotion of political dominance, and total stranglehold on the new country exacted for extreme exclusion of oppressed populations in the country. These failures in leadership are the sole triggers of uprooting populations from their ancestral lands in the agriculture heartlands of South Sudan, particularly in Equatoria – blunders perpetuated for expansionist tribal drives, committed with impunity under watch of those misruling the country.

The ongoing weaponised tribal campaigns against politically marginalised populations have caused unparalleled loss of lives and devastation of the country's human potential to unimaginable proportions and to deeply worrying levels. More devastated by the internal war are women, children, and the politically marginalised populations. Sadly, these outrageous crimes against humanity are alarming signs of state dismantling.

To withstand the calculated assaults on our hard-earned freedom, the people of South Sudan should rally together to stop the current promotion of negative ethnicity. The prevailing mindset of those at the top bent on total democratic exclusion and expulsion of oppressed populations from their ancestral lands must be ended forthwith. Getting rid of extreme misrule and impunity is the way forward to following a peaceful path towards building the nation state desired by all.

All of us together will gain more from standing firm and united against the political upheavals that reduced the country to its present fragility. However, any turnaround of fortunes in the land must begin with the country's current rulers accepting that they have seriously let down the people of South Sudan.

Actions taken by the warmongers to make amends for the heinous crimes they inflicted on the people of South Sudan must start with renunciation of violence as a means of resolving conflicts. To accomplish that goal, those in power should rise above tribal proclivities, partisan politics, and vested interests as a way forward for proper address of the root causes of the internal strife, and above all by committing themselves to promotion of sustainable peace.

Given the entrenched divisive politics and the outrageous ethnic divisions generated in the past to date in South Sudan, there is a dire need for establishment of a national order – one that must be based on the rule of law and democratic participation. Current rulers in the country must give way to the next generation of leaders, personalities worthy of people's trust to run the country.

The search of rightful leaders to propel the country to a peaceful and viable nation state is a must-do assignment – governance high hurdles that should be confronted now, not tomorrow. For realisation of those goals, lessons should be drawn from past efforts of our pioneer leaders who mobilised our people towards the nation-state idea.

To replicate that legacy, men and women with outstanding leadership qualities should be employed for conveyance of compelling ideas and promotion of messages of peace. Such leadership qualities are critically needed for restoration of people's broken lives – an impetus for getting our young country back on the development track. New and inspired leaders are required for realisation of these human development goals.

In addressing the education and development needs of the younger generation, the basis for proper exploitation of our human potential must be laid down properly. In that way our youths' sense of self-worth and interest in pursuing their education and development goals will have been enhanced. Such approaches in socio-economic development will greatly assist them to ready their human potential for post-conflict recovery and development of South Sudan.

In recounting some of these lifelong experiences in this letter, dear children, I am attempting to convey to you all that any turnaround of fortunes in the motherland is possible, but one that must be attained after our bleeding country is steered out of darkness.

Dear my children, and the rest of the younger generation in our war-torn country, I recognise the hardships you endured and continue to face, ills brought upon you by us, the older generation. For those of you who have attained your education goals, you have ridden your development storms through hard times. Your resolve to reach the top is not dented by the horrendous failings of the present times.

For those of you forced out of learning by acts of violence, war, and extreme neglect of your education needs, you have shown that your resolve to succeed remains undisturbed. Your fortitude, resilience, and focus on whatever you do to improve yourselves is recognised and hailed in this letter.

The staggering leadership blunders have brought upon you all untold misery. Those in power have robbed you of your wealth resources; mortgaged your future, freedom, and existence; and are presently misruling the country to total fragility. You must be told about these failings to prepare yourselves well for what is awaiting you. You must shape a better future for yourselves out of the silver lining in the dark clouds.

Despite the devastations of the prolonged political conflicts in the country, and the immeasurable human loss that impacted the country in the past and currently, these harrowing misfortunes should motivate you to be more focused in the pursuance of your education and personal development, as a means of contributing towards the march to total freedom in South Sudan.

Draw lessons from our past experiences and struggles, anchors that should keep you dreaming for an optimistic future. Staying connected on that path will keep you in good stead now and in the future.

The way forward in South Sudan must be drawn from some of the lessons and experiences outlined above, and from many more sources out there that will definitely come your way. Grab the liberty torch, run the relay race, and complete the unfinished march to freedom.

18

Be Proud of the Greatness that You Are

My Dear Children,

Tracing your hard education journey, I recognise the learning struggles that you surmounted – hardships that prepared you well to earn the accolades you accomplished. Well done for those achievements that you attained despite the past and the present uncertainties, which did not dissuade you from realisation of your education and development dreams.

Remember, we, your parents, stood by you in following your education and career pursuits. We are watching over you in whatever you do under guidance of our ancestors, the patriarchs, and matriarchs of this family.

Given your drive to succeed in whatever you do, each one of you will reach the top like mahogany trees perched on top of highest mountains. Remaining focused in that way, you will reach other lofty heights in your professions and careers. And if you face difficulties in reaching those mountaintops after one or several attempts, don't give up trying because you will reach that end.

Rise up to complete the journey. "Your greatest glory is not in never falling, but in rising each time you fall." I didn't say that. Confucius said it many centuries ago, a relevant mantra applicable to this day.

Your resilience and fortitude in the pursuance of your ideals have paid off. Celebrate every step you make and continue to do good to yourselves and your loved ones, our grandchildren.

My beloved children, everything you need to be happy and successful is already inside of you – potentialities that moulded you to what you are. We, your parents, are very proud to be a small part of the greatness that you are.

This book is printed on paper from sustainable sources managed under the Forest Stewardship Council (FSC) scheme.

It has been printed in the UK to reduce transportation miles and their impact upon the environment.

For every new title that Troubador publishes, we plant a tree to offset CO_2, partnering with the More Trees scheme.

For more about how Troubador offsets its environmental impact, see www.troubador.co.uk/sustainability-and-community